The Strongest One of All

based on a Caucasian folktale

Mirra Ginsburg

pictures by
Jose Aruego & Ariane Dewey

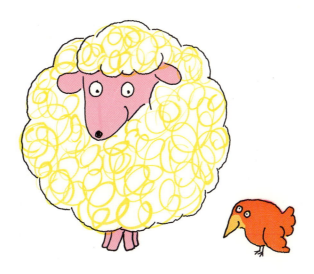

Greenwillow Books

A Division of William Morrow & Company, Inc., New York

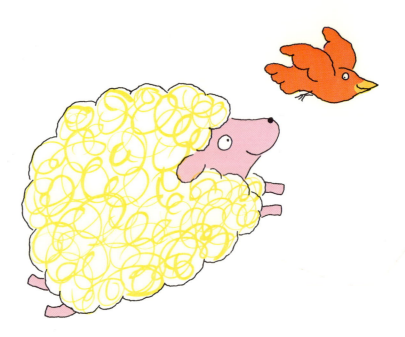

Library of Congress Cataloging in Publication Data

Ginsburg, Mirra.   The strongest one of all.
Summary: A lamb asks the ice, sun, cloud,
rain, earth, and grass who is the strongest one
of all and reaches a surprising conclusion.
[1. Folklore—Caucasus] I. Aruego, Jose.
II. Dewey, Ariane. III. Title. PZ8.1.G455ST [E]
76-44326   ISBN 0-688-80081-5 ISBN 0-688-84081-7 lib. bdg.

To Polya
—M.G.

To Juan
—A.D. & J.A.

A lamb slipped on the ice and cried,

"Ice, ice, you made me fall.
Are you strong?
Are you the strongest one of all?"

But the ice answered,
"If I were the strongest,
would the sun melt me?"

The lamb went to the sun and asked,

"Sun, sun,
   are you the strongest one of all?"

But the sun answered,
"If I were the strongest,
would the cloud cover me?"

The lamb went to the cloud and asked,
"Cloud, cloud,
are you the strongest one of all?"

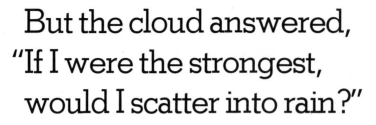

But the cloud answered,
"If I were the strongest,
would I scatter into rain?"

The lamb went to the rain and asked,
"Rain, rain,
   are you the strongest one of all?"

But the rain answered,
"If I were the strongest,
would the earth swallow me?"

The lamb went to the earth and asked,
"Earth, earth,
  are you the strongest one of all?"

But the earth answered,
"If I were the strongest,
would the grass push its roots
down through me,
push its shoots
up through me?"

The lamb went to the grass and asked,
"Grass, grass,
    are you the strongest one of all?"

But the grass answered,
"If I were the strongest,
would a lamb pluck me,

would a lamb eat me?"

And the lamb leaped with joy.
"I may slip, and I may fall,
but I'm the strongest!
I'm the strongest of them all!"